Worsh

Small Congregations

by
David Cutts
Rector of Coddenham with Gosbeck and Hemingstone with Henley,
diocese of St. Edmundsbury and Ipswich

GROVE BOOKS LIMITED
Bramcote   Nottingham   NG9 3DS

CONTENTS

THE COVER PICTURE

is by Peter Ashton, and is part of a larger cartoon used on both covers of No 82 in this series.

First Impression April 1989

ISBN 0144-1728
ISBN 1 85174 109 7

1. WHERE TWO OR THREE

Every week some people attend church services where there are only a handful present. For some this is just what they want. For example being in a country church can be delightful. The sun streaming in through the windows and the quietness outside help create a deep sense of peace. The fact that there are only a few people there seems to emphasize the spaciousness of the countryside. Calmness and tranquillity are the dominant feelings.

However come winter in such a place then the situation is very different and might be something like this . . .:

> Two hundred people live in the sprawling village of Hereton under River. For 'pastoral reasons'[1] the Church of England parish is grouped with three others under one vicar who lives in Hereton-over-River which is five miles away from Hereton-under-River. There is a service every week at the large church building on the edge of the village, though not at the same time each Sunday. This week the vicar will be coming himself to take Evensong. Because it is the middle of February he isn't expecting many worshippers.[2]
>
> When he arrives fifteen minutes before the service is due to begin there are no other cars outside the church and no lights on anywhere. Fortunately the vicar has brought his torch and can therefore find the door and equally vitally the light switch. The church is cold and the vicar can see his own breath. He switches the church heaters on and goes into the vestry and lights the candle that is needed in there due to the lack of electricity.
>
> In time five others arrive, one of whom is the organist. He does his best with the four hymns but clearly has difficulty in playing tunes with a key signature of three or more flats. As a concession to the low numbers the vicar announces that they will say the psalm but still sing the canticles. Otherwise the service proceeds as normal though the vicar wonders about saying 'as many as are here present' in the introduction to the Confession.
>
> One of the congregation agrees to read one of the lessons and apart from stumbling over some of the names he does quite well. Unfortunately his quiet voice is lost in the vastness of the building and only the vicar can hear what he is saying. The members of the congregation haven't helped by all sitting in the back three pews, as far away from each other as possible.

[1] This phrase is sometimes used as a euphemism to describe the declining number of clergy in rural areas.

[2] Weather is often given as an explanation for low numbers at a church service. Thus it is said in July that everyone has gone out for the day because the sun is shining. Realism is vital in any discussion about numbers in worship. For example in a village of 200 a congregation of 10 is an achievement.

The vicar tries to make the sermon relevant to the people there but he finds this difficult to do without sounding as if he is 'getting at' them individually. He believes that the whole business is rather feeble and he cannot comprehend why they each thank him at the door for such a lovely service.

Unknown yet to those in church the vicar will be leaving them soon, having accepted the Bishop's invitation to become vicar of a thriving urban parish. There fifty are expected at the evening service and over two hundred will normally be present in the morning. His enthusiasm for rural ministry has waned after just two years ...

This description of a service may seem unrealistic but sadly for many in the church today there will be a ring of truth.

There are three situations in mind. Firstly there are those churches where the service with a small congregation is the only act of worship in that place on that particular Sunday. This could be a rural setting or does occur in many urban parishes.

Secondly there are services with few people present when there will be other weekly occasions at which a crowd is expected. For example, where there is a thriving Sunday morning Parish Communion, there may well be small numbers at an earlier celebration at 8 a.m., at Evensong at 6.30 p.m. the same day, at the Daily Office during the week, and at midweek and saints' days communion services.

Lastly there are various places where the number present at worship is inevitably small; such as homes for the elderly, hospital chapels and religious communities.

This booklet will concentrate on the first category but may be of interest to people involved in the other situations. The author's present sphere of ministry is rural and this has obviously influenced much of what is written here. There is already in this series of booklets something on worship in Urban Priority Areas[1] though this does not mean that this booklet excludes such parishes in its thinking.

Firstly we consider what is the relevance and appropriateness of services where there are only a few present. This discussion is vital because without some underlying belief in what is happening a small congregation will quickly lose heart. It is hoped that the Archbishop's Commission on Rural Areas (ACORA) will firmly address this issue in its deliberations on worship.[2]

---

[1] John Bentham *Worship in the City* (Grove Books, 1986).
[2] Its urban equivalent *Faith in the City* did not seem to give sufficient emphasis to this.

2. SOME PRINCIPLES

1. How small is too small?

Much of the modern theory about the life of the church concentrates on the desirability of sub-dividing a church community into groups of about a dozen. It is assumed that a viable church has that need. In other words that there is a congregation large enough to benefit from such subdivision. Warnings may be issued against a church having too many numbers[1] but rarely is there any examination of the underlying assumption that there are already over one hundred present.

This may seem curious when we consider how the church first prospered. Part of the background of the early life of the church was the synagogue. Some of the first converts from the Jewish faith would have been used to the idea of their regular worship in small numbers, not through choice but through necessity. A synagogue only needed ten men to be the charter members and even when that minimum was not achieved some sort of meeting for worship was still possible.[2]

When the persecution of Christians generally halted in the Fourth Century buildings began to spring up all over the place. Until then the believers had been used to worshipping in someone's home, possibly in secret. Numbers must have been restricted by necessity.

In addition, throughout the Christian age it has been accepted that families can and do function as a worshipping unit. It has been thought natural for a household to gather for prayer and Bible reading.[3] Today many families sing hymns and choruses together without questioning what they are doing. In this Grove Worship Series the booklet on 'Family Festivals' is sub-titled 'An Approach to Family *Worship'*.[4] All this seems perfectly reasonable. However, when a similar number gather in a church building many will not consider that meeting to be appropriate as an opportunity for genuine worship. Indeed when I accepted my present post some of my urban colleagues tried to tell me that leading small numbers in worship was a waste of time; being a country incumbent was not a proper job; it would be better for the few to travel to the nearest town for their worship.

My assertion is that there is no logic in thinking that some particular number is the minimum for a viable church community. Instead it is preferable to consider whether there is a particular civic community or part of

---

[1] See for example Eddie Gibbs, *I believe in Church Growth,* (Hodder, 1981) ch 7. On p. 279 a church of less than 150 members is described as a small church. Some of us would think anything over 80 is big!

[2] See Acts 16.13.

[3] Various examples could be cited including the well known prayer life of the Little Gidding Community. For more details see the author's joint publication with Harold Miller *Whose Office? Daily Prayer for the People of God* (Grove Books, 1982) p28f.

[4] Grove Worship Series no 73 compiled by Michael Vasey and others. My italics in the sub-title.

a community to which the church fellowship can relate. In the Church of England this has been traditionally the local parish, whether as the whole of a civic parish or part of a town or city. Even villages which have a small population have their own parish church. There is therefore this natural civic community for the church to interact with and to serve.

In a village community there is also the concept of 'maintaining the presence'. It is argued that the physical existence of a church building says something about the active presence of God in that community. Critics of this view say that the church building gives all the wrong impressions such as a church more concerned with bricks and mortar than with a living Christian faith, a church of people who love the building more than they love the Lord. There may be something in this but a redundant church hardly gives the right impression either.[1]

A small congregation then may feel it worthwhile to meet for worship in a building the villagers are working to keep in good repair. This sense of purpose may be stretched to the limit however when an incumbent and two others (one of whom arrived late) meet in a cold rural church on a winter's evening. The feeling of 'what are we doing here' is natural. What is often wrong is the manner of worshipping, not the concept of being together as the church community in that geographical area. We therefore need to discover (or possibly rediscover) what works and what is best discarded.

2. For what purpose do we come together?

The obvious aim of any gathering of Christian people in a church building is to worship. That worship is truly a response, a recognition of all that God is and has done and is doing. It is meant to be a natural response of God's created and redeemed people. Just as this is possible for an individual it must also be true for a small gathering. After all our Lord has promised his presence amongst the group on such occasions![2]

This central theme of the worship of God must dominate any gathering of the community for a church service. There will be questions that have to asked about the style and content of such services and particularly how best they can satisfy those who come. However care must be taken to avoid losing sight of this chief aim.

3. How important are the personal needs of the worshippers?

It would be foolish to pretend that those who gather together come perfectly prepared for worship as if somehow they have left their personalities at home.

In a small congregation this is particularly accentuated. The single parent with a small child may be looking for support and understanding from the congregation. She may be hoping that the church service will sufficiently occupy her child so that she can, for once, relax a little. The business executive and his wife, staying in their weekend cottage may be looking

---

[1] The financial burden of this is discussed below on p.15.
[2] Matthew 18.20. Note the use of this phrase in the Prayer of St Chrysostom, set in the Book of Common Prayer order for Morning and Evening Prayer. In the contrast to the introduction to the confession, mentioned above on p.3, this part of the service sounds fine with a small congregation!

for peace and a sense of stability in the service, a welcome break from their hectic weekly schedule. In a church expecting large numbers these conflicting needs will on the one hand be absorbed by the provision of a creche or on the other by the opportunity to attend an early morning communion. In a small setting without such provision the conflict will be only too apparent.

The resultant pressures on those who lead the worship can be devastating. In a large congregation if the leader decides to follow a particular line then he may lose some to other, nearby churches. This may be regrettable but those who come in will probably compensate. If, out of a congregation of less than ten, two families go off in a huff there is a very significant change in the whole nature of what is possible.

4. What should be the general approach?

In the end the way forward must be to assess realistically what is appropriate for the various regular worshippers and try to provide a pattern of services over a month which will cater for this diversity, yet without losing the possibility of attracting new people. Weekly attendance at church may be thought to be essential but may not be prudent. My own view now is that it is better to try and provide for the varied tastes in worship once a month than attempting to force everyone to do the same thing. With this as a starting point I would suggest the goal to keep firmly in view is the time when all can worship together every week as the family of God in that place. Realistically though many small congregations are a long way from that.

Initial acceptance of the situation is essential because it builds up confidence in the existing congregation. After a good period of listening[1] by those involved in ministry then there is every hope that the church will be able to move forward together and explore some new pastures together. This is a radical change of approach for many clergy if they have been trained to work in parishes where large congregations are expected (and probably came from such a church in the first place). In those circumstances their expectation may well be for 'something to happen' quickly. Of course some have come to the country and made sweeping changes from the start. For a short period things go well but curiously such clergy seem to move on quickly, leaving a church unable to cope without them.

If a local congregation can be encouraged to be realistic about their situation then they will also need to be gently trained to worship within the constraints that small numbers imply. This is partly to do with helping people to have reasonable expectations but also to see that they have a part to play as well.

The following chapter considers a range of particular features of small congregations, seeking to put these principles into practice. Most of the issues are presented as problems to be solved, though, of course, not all small congregations will be faced by all of them!

[1] This being years rather than months.

3. PRINCIPLES INTO PRACTICE

A strong sense of community

In many of the areas of the country where there are small congregations there may be some sense of community spirit. Thus in a village there may be a general acceptence that the residents have something in common simply due to the fact that they live in the same civic parish. In an Urban Priority Area the common experiences of poverty, unemployment etc may be considered to be a unifying factor.

This community feeling may in part be an illusion. In urban areas the community may be split by racial tensions, different lifestyles, the type of housing in which people live etc. Perhaps the topical split is now between the 'Yuppies' and what is left of the indigeneous population. In agricultural areas farmers, old villagers and new villagers may be distinct groups.[1] However sharp these divisions are there still may be a sense of community in so far that people have a desire to believe that a commom community spirit exists. It is not inappropriate to use this sense of community to enhance the worship.

For example if those coming together believe that they have a ministry to intercede for the wider community then it will give a definite aim to parts of the service such as the intercessions. The norm may be the use of a few vague, general prayers covering issues unrelated to the few there. By focusing on the local community there can be genuine prayer for people, places and situations.

It may be that there are those amongst the few who, with encouragement, can be asked to lead the intercessions. If that is too much to aim for there is no reason why boxes should not be provided for people to deposit prayer requests on slips of paper. Alternatively at the appropriate point in the service the congregation could be asked to suggest items for prayer.

These latter ideas call now for courage on behalf of the leader. The requests may seem flippant or irrelevant or not forthcoming at all. Somehow they will have to be gathered into a meaningful prayer. The aim though is important—the practicalities will come.

Divisions in the community

In any community the church group may well be the only organization which includes people from the various groups. The apostle Paul's call for unity[2] is just as applicable today, though the divisions may have changed.

The church in a divided community can immediately be a place of the healing of these differences. For example in a rural area where people divide

---

[1] See Anthony Russell, *The Country Parish,* (SPCK,1986) for a fascinating analysis of these groupings. It is important to distinquish between agricultural and mining villages for instance since the groupings will vary.
[2] Galatians 3.28.

up into the groups mentioned previously[1] a small gathering of some from each can visibly demonstrate some hope of unity. There can be genuine intercession about the causes of the divisions with action reaching out to the community from that starting point.

Depression

In the introduction to this booklet a depressing situation was portrayed in a slighty farcical fashion but may well have 'rung bells' for some readers. Worship in small numbers can be very disheartening for both the leaders and the congregation, especially where there was once a larger number present or where the few have happy memories of big congregations elsewhere.

Realism is essential. It is fruitless to expect continually that large numbers will one day come if only something particular happened. Acceptance of the situation will help a great deal and can readily lead onto mutual support and encouragement. False heartiness, continual complaining, constant harking back to the 'good old days' are not helpful and must be discouraged by all involved.

Nostalgia

The Church of England is steeped in tradition but sometimes the 'old days' hang ominously over all that is done. A friend of mine in a large market town parish was told that in the past over three hundred had regularly attended evensong which compared somewhat unfavourably with his experience of less than ten. The implication was that his ministry was not successful compared with that of his predecessors and that if only he would adopt the views and approaches of those days many would flock into the service.[2] After suffering so much of this he examined old church service registers and discovered the average at the time in question to be thirty, larger numbers coming only at major festivals.

On the other hand the past is important to people, and not just the elderly. Many of us have happy memories of services we attended during our childhood and even though our recollection may have become imprecise with the passage of time there may be lessons to learn about what might work well in any given situation.

The appropriate approach to nostalgia is to listen carefully to whatever is said with an attempt to discern what the reality might have been. Confrontation rarely works but the telling of such stories as that above may illuminate peoples' conception of how we recall the past.

Possibly the hardest area is the idea that far more people came to church in the past. Records may help as above but in the end we may simply have to live with the fact that this is what people think and use such comments to encourage people to bring others along now. The 'where is everyone else' syndrome is linked closely with the depression that both ministers and congregations experience.

[1] See above p. 8.
[2] I should point out that the weekly Family Communion is very well attended.

Another example from a local parish illustrates this point. A parish magazine contained recollections of the past. One parishioner had written of the days when 'everyone in the village attended church every Sunday morning' and 'woe betide anyone who was missing—the parson would be round to call later that week'. This cannot possibly be true since the church in question holds at a pinch three hundred, the population of the village at the time being about one thousand. A more rational analysis would come to the conclusion that many of the people of a particular social group would have been at Mattins, others would have been preparing the lunch for them! The sociological situation was vastly different and bears little relation to church attendance today.

Part of this desire to quote the past is because the life then seemed to be so good and therefore there is a tendency to romanticize about it. Note for example the continued popularity of such works as *Kilvert's Diary*— though it should be said that a realistic reading of such a work paints a far from rosy picture.[1] Again Bishop Anthony Russell's works give helpful insights into the past.[2]

Church Growth

Church growth is a very real and exciting prospect[3] in a small congregation, provided the expectations of those involved are realistic. One new member in a church which started the year with ten people is 10% growth. How many large congregations can match that! Or, as mentioned above[4] a congregation of 5% is good in any area of the country and it must be realized that 5% of a parish with a small population is very few people.

Also it is important not to become obsessed with figures. It can be very daunting for a congregation to feel that they are being counted each week[5], not just for statistical purposes but because the leaders of the local church put great store on how many are there each week. A large congregation can absorb fluctuations due to illness, holidays etc because they tend to even themselves out. If three people are missing for a month out of a usual gathering of ten then it might be thought that something serious had happened.

Resistance to change

Change in any institution is often hard to effect. The church in particular seems to suffer from an often extreme resistance which can make any worthwhile leader despair of seeing any growth.

Part of this presumably is the sense that God is unchanging therefore anything which is overtly to do with God must remain as it always has been. This view makes God seem remote and static as if he has no contact with

---

[1] The entry for December 3rd 1871 reveals that Kilvert had problems with small congregations too! See William Plomer (ed.), *Kilvert's Diary*, (Penguin, 1977).
[2] Anthony Russell, *op. cit.* and *The Clerical Profession*, (SPCK, 1980).
[3] See John Richardson (ed.), *Ten Rural Churches*, (MARC, 1988) for some encouraging stories of what has happened in some rural situations.
[4] See above page 3.
[5] Such a count is strictly necessary in the Church of England for the annual return of church membership, required by the Central Board of Finance.

his creation. A more appropriate view sees an unchanging God at work in an ever-changing world. The gospel therefore can be seen to be as traditionally viewed by the church. The method of proclamation in mission, presentation in worship and realization in behaviour must vary and be strictly contemporary if the church is to be relevant.

Persuading a small group of regular worshippers of this can be extremely difficult. It may seem amazing that people who readily accept change in virtually every other area of their lives find it so hard to cope with the slightest alteration to a church service. They may well sit at the Church Council meeting wearing digital watches, and then drive home in 'F' registration cars to watch a previously recorded programme on their colour television. Such acceptance of the 1980s will not persuade them at that meeting that a new hymn book or to have a monthly service at which children will feel welcome are changes which they should encourage.

It is essential in such circumstances to thoroughly analyse the reasons for such resistance. Until such underlying thought patterns are perceived suggestion of change will only produce further resistance. There are many possibilities. Perhaps the person was married at the church or had their children baptised there. Thus any change to the fabric which will alter the appearance of the building may subconsciously imply something about the security of their family life. Or perhaps the person has moved to the countryside as a haven from the busyness of urban life. Any desire to include children in church may suggest noise and disturbance.

The next stage is perhaps the hardest. The individuals involved need to be seen as individuals and carefully and lovingly encouraged to face the real issues in their own lives. For example consideration would need to be given to whether the desire for a haven expresses some inability to cope with life as it is. There is no short cut to this and many frustrations will follow.

The eventual aim must be to help people to cope with the present and to bring that present into their worship. It does not necessarily follow that every new fashion in liturgy has to be accepted! Instead a genuine appreciation of the past and all that it has to offer will lead to a greater awareness of how God has been at work in his world which in turn enables people to see how he can work in the present.

Small is beautiful

Some of those who attend services with small numbers will be very pleased to find only a few present. Some may have chosen not to worship in their own parish church but rather travel some distance to a smaller set up where they can be noticed and made to feel important. Others are looking for a service where numbers are small because this may well mean an absence of hearty worship.

All these concepts can be used positively without betraying the basic principles of a gospel that is meant to be shared and of a church that is there to grow. The peace and quiet of a rural church may well be a haven for all those who come. That can be built on with the silence used creatively. The need to be important is a basic human need. Used positively this can bring the individual to a place where his importance is seen in terms of his own personal calling by God to a particular ministry in the church.

Individual religion

Part of the culture shock of the modern language services was the expression they gave to the idea that the church is a corporate body.[1] It would be an over-simplification to suggest that until then no one was aware of this but certainly many would have expressed their attendance at Communion services in terms of 'making *my* communion'.

In a small congregation such attitudes can be very divisive partly because the desire for personal satisfaction becomes dominant. Church members need to be challenged with the New Testament teaching on the concept of the Church as the body of Christ and made aware of the implications for them in that particular situation. The danger is that such teaching consists of some vague generalizations which reveal the preacher's lack of experience in the setting in which he now finds himself. If the minister's personal Christian training has been in large churches this will quite subconsciously affect his preaching and he may be exhorting his congregation to an inappropriate concept of the church.

Buildings

It is tempting to suggest that church buildings are rarely the right size! On the one hand a thriving church community finds itself bulging at the seams of a small building[2] whilst at the the other extreme the few who come are spaced out in a huge, cold medieval 'treasure'.[3] The first problem is really beyond the brief of this particular booklet and for those in leadership in areas of low church attendance it must seem like a joy not a problem. The second problem is a very real one in many urban and rural situations and needs sensitive as well as creative handling. Part of the problem is that a large building seems to imply that a large number should come.

The major difficulty to surmount may well be to do with the previously discussed 'individual religion'.[4] Leaders of worship may want everyone to sit reasonably close together because it makes it easier to lead the act of

---

[1] Take for example the introduction to the Nicene Creed—'We believe . . .' How many of the opponents of this change realized that this was the original wording?

[2] This can happen in rural areas as well as urban especially where a village has expanded rapidly in population in recent years.

[3] I suspect that some buildings have always been too big. In other words the population of the village has never been sufficient to fill the church even if everyone had come.

[4] See above on this page.

worship as well as being an expression of the corporate nature of the church. The sermon can be directed in one direction, the singing is likely to be better since the few voices encourage one another, the parts which are said by all sound more convincing and so on. However this view of the need for 'togetherness' will not be shared by everyone. People will sit where they do in church for various reasons. They may find that particular 'view' condusive to worship, they may have sat there for many years, they may have sat there with other members of their family who have since died or moved away, they may be able to see the door and thus who comes and goes, there may be an absence of draughts where they are, they may be near a heater, they may like to be near the door and feel agoraphobic[1] elsewhere etc. It is only too easy for others to scoff at these reasons which merely makes the people more determined to stay where they are because they feel that they are not being understood.

One sound piece of advice given to me was 'if they will not come nearer the front, then pursue them down the church'! This raises all sorts of possibilities including taking intercessions from the back of the church, even leading much of Mattins or Evensong from the back (and therefore also enjoying the view and the warmth as well), walking up and down the nave during the sermon and using 'forward altars'.

I find this sort of approach to be more helpful than trying to move the congregation virtually by force. In particular many do find our old buildings to be an inspiration to their worship and therefore the 'view' is important. It is better to build on this sense of the numinous than insensitively destroying it.

Some congregations, of course, will find various forms of reordering their church to be helpful. There are at least three motives for this: liturgical needs, catering for fellowship requirements or a desire to keep the heating bills down. It is beyond the scope of this booklet to go into detail[1] except to say that it is nearly always a good idea to go and view other churches where they have undertaken such work, preferably where the situation in the parish is similar. In the Church of England, the Diocesan Advisory Committee will have details of these as well as being able to give advice about what is possible.

The neighbouring church

When a church is faced with some of the difficulties mentioned above then it is only too easy to think that no-one else quite has these problems. And yet a realistic assessment of other local churches (including other denominations) makes it clear that many other churches have the same sort of problems. There are two useful opportunities here.

Firstly there must be some sense in joining together on occasions, provided that it is not so frequent that the sense of the church community

---

[1] I understand that this is a very real problem for some people. Presumably others may sit near the door in a small church for exactly the opposite reason.

community ministering to a particular area is lost. It would be good for church unity, both within ones own denomination and with others. At base level it will provide a larger congregation which all should enjoy. However this does not always come about easily. For example many rural groups of parishes have tried to hold joint services on fifth Sundays, or on a monthly basis or even weekly. It seems that those who go rejoice at being part of a larger set-up for a change but there will be some, probably many, who will stay at home if the service is not in their own church.

Part of this problem must be the very real fear that too much contact with others will bring about a loss of identity. If joint services become too frequent it will be thought that the next stage will be all joint services followed eventually by closure of all but one of the churches in the group. Perhaps a comparable situation is to consider the links that many small schools form. There is no loss of identity at all but the children benefit greatly from common sports days, outings, class work etc.

The second opportunity here is learning from others' experiences. Clergy and ministers can talk about common problems though unfortunately 'professional pride' too often prevents this. Also conferences can be arranged for interested people, again to share together in wrestling with the vital questions of the church's ministry in the areas in question.

Sitting in the shadow of the larger concern

The question of the nearby well-filled church as an alternative place of worship for parishioners is a perpetual issue for a small congregation. Many such congregations feel highly threatened by this especially when there is a tendency for the cream of the local believers to go off every Sunday to attend for example a strong evangelical, charismatic church rather than their local church. The temptation to do this is very strong, particularly for those who have worshipped in such churches before they moved out to a country area. The issues behind this need to be understood by both sides. On the one hand the local church will never flourish if the potential leaders go elsewhere. On the other hand it is natural to want to worship in a lively atmosphere, with plenty of people, especially if there are children in the family with a need to be part of suitable activities for their age group.

The most helpful attitude to this problem, I believe, is to accept it and not try to fight against it. One possibility is to encourage people in such situations to worship once a month in their local parish church. Thus the local community has a chance to benefit from the gifts which these people have to offer without preventing them participating more regularly in the sort of worship they feel they need.

In addition it can be helpful to seek to form a more positive link with the larger church. There have been attempts to 'twin' inner-city parishes with

[1] See two booklets by Kenneth White, *Centres for the Servants,* (Grove Books, 1975) and *The Attractive Church,* (Grove Books, 1979), both being out of print. Also the magazine *Church Building* has details of many such schemes.

churches elsewhere and provided the aims are clear this can be of mutual benefit. Similarly a rural parish could form such a bond with an urban parish in a nearby town. On the one hand the rural parish can offer the space and quiet of the countryside. On the other the large urban parish will have manpower resources which can be of help and encouragement to the few meeting in the country church.

Money problems

Small numbers almost certainly will produce small collections. Keeping a church building in good repair therefore can become an almost overwhelming burden, yet this burden cannot be released easily. The buildings in many cases have stood there for centuries and if our ancestors provided them for us have we the right to fail to pass them on to those who follow?

This is particularly important in villages because so often the church is the only community building left, now that the school has closed and the public house and shop found to be uneconomical to run. Few numbers in church now give no clue to what might happen in the future. In one of the villages I serve congregations were very small at one time. In the last thirty years many new houses have been built around the church and our monthly Family Communion attracts about 70 people. The temptation to close such a church could have been strong in the past. Now it could be considered to be too small for the village!

As so often before there must be a great sense of realism underlying this. It is tempting to covet one's neighbours church extensions or internal re-ordering but the prime need is to concentrate on what is actually possible. If the weekly offerings are small then other methods of fund raising must be sought.

If the sense of parish identity is strong, such as in a village, then a sensitive approach to the parish as a whole is appropriate. Many people will consider favourably an appeal for regular donations provided they are able to see where the money is going. Fund raising events can be enjoyable and also are an opportunity to involve others in the life of the church. If a weekend of special events ends with a service in church the attendance is likely to be good.

The services leading up to the event can be used as preparation giving valuable prayer support to the organisers and opening opportunities for people to see the events in an evangelistic sense.

The place of children

The number of children present in the sort of situations which we are examining is by definition likely to be very small. We may find, for example, that there are three children present as part of a congregation of twenty and the children's ages are three, seven and eleven.

There are many problems related to this. How is the service to be made relevant to the children? How can the sermon be of interest to them and to the other seventeen there? If the youngest child is restless will she distract the congregation so much that those who came for peace and quiet find exactly the opposite? How can the minister plan adequately for the service not knowing if there are going to be children present until they arrive at the church?

The first point is to stress the appropriateness of the children being there. As baptized members of the body of Christ they have as much right as anyone else to be present and to participate in the service. This simple statement is extremely difficult for some congregations to accept and realism may dictate that it is made clear that some services are more suitable for children than others. However, occasional reminders of the wording of the Alternative Sevice Book Baptism service may help—'we welcome you into the Lord's family . . .'

Secondly adult members of the congregation need to appreciate that children's needs and attitudes are very different today from those of their own children or themselves. Remarks such as 'my children were always made to behave in church' are unhelpful because they have no bearing on today's situation. It is salutory to inquire sometimes in response to such remarks as to how often those once well-behaved children now attend church!

Children today need highly visual activities in which they can participate by self-expression. Much of the teaching in schools now functions on those lines and the days of sitting in rows, copying from the board, are thankfully gone. If children are experiencing a different environment at school then shouldn't this change be reflected in church?

In any church service there can be a great deal of activity and children should be encouraged to be part of it. They could help prepare the building for worship, getting books out, lighting candles (under supervision!), preparing the altar for communion[1] and so on. As the service starts they could lead the minister to his place from the vestry if there is no choir, at communion services form a gospel procession (possibly with lighted candles depending on their ages) and so on.

There will be some discussion of music later[2] but children's needs must be borne in mind, especially since many adults enjoy choruses (with actions!).

The sermon perhaps presents the biggest hurdle. In a large building the children could be given some material to work through which relates to the theme whilst the adults listen to the spoken word. However in a small building this is virtually impossible. Children find it easier to listen if there are visual aids and interesting examples. I try occasionally to use an example which may amuse the children and then leave the adults to think through the implications for themselves.

[1] There is no reason at all why children should not do this and they will quite naturally learn to be reverent in a way that other worshippers will appreciate. Alternatively this all could be done during the offertory hymn.
[2] See below pp.17f.

All the above relates to Sunday services. There is of course scope for midweek activities which include worship. Many churches have had successful 'pram services' or combined with a mothers and toddlers group. Various factors need to be born in mind. The building must be warm.[1] The service must be short, with plenty of involvement for the children. The language must not only be appropriate for the children but also for any mums who are not used to church services!

Newcomers and Visitors

Visitors to a church service can be very noticeable where there are normally only a few present. It is not that they are unwelcome, though this sadly might be the case, but rather that the whole dynamic of the worship changes, partly because the leader is unprepared for this eventuality. There is no easy remedy to this. It sounds useful always to bear in mind that newcomers *might* turn up—and plan the service accordingly—but this is hardly realistic. In the end it may be that the style and presentation of the worship will have to change on the day rather than the ingredients. This is difficult to achieve without experience but is a helpful quality to cultivate in the leadership of worship in general.

Music

There are two areas to consider here. Firstly there is a question of what is the best instrument to use for leading the singing with a small congregation and secondly there is the question of what they should sing.

Most if not all churches are supplied with an organ, though with a wide variety in types. Questions are sometimes asked about the suitability of this instrument for leading singing since the note it gives is not clear enough for some. The debate is sharpened in a church where few come because there may not be someone able to play the organ.

There are various possibilies. Firstly someone who can play the piano may be persuaded to play the organ after some simple instruction from an experienced organist about the use of stops. The pianist needs to be encouraged to accept that it is not necessary to be able to play the full harmony. A recent publication is a great help in this.[2] In time the pianist can be offered the chance to go on a course to improve his organ technique further.

If this is not possible then alternative sorts of instrumentation need to be investigated. A recorder gives a clear note though the usual descant instrument is an octave higher then expected. The advantage of using this is that many people can play a recorder and particularly many children. I have led singing myself in this way in the open air and know it works! Offers of other instruments need to be investigated carefully! I am not

---

[1] It is surprising how accepting congregations become of low temperatures in church. Such lack of warmth is quite unacceptable for activities involving young children.

[2] Janette Cooper *Hymns Tunes for the Reluctant Organist* (OUP,1987). Speaking as someone who can just about play the piano I find this book to be very helpful, both in its advice and in its arrangements of a selection of well-known hymn tunes.

musically competent to judge which type of instrument would be good and which less than helpful but it is obvious that some are hard to play well enough to give a confident lead.

The guitar may sound appealing but there are difficulties. Firstly most guitarists are actually offering a series of chords rather than a specific and distinct note to sing. Secondly in my experience guitar accompanied singing only works well when the person playing the guitar is a confident enough singer to start everyone off. Thirdly in a large building nylon strung guitars cannot be heard!

Some churches now used 'canned music' in either of two senses. One possibility is for various hymn tunes to be recorded during the previous week by a good organist. The tape can then be reproduced and taken wherever is necessary for the Sunday worship. I have no personal experience of this but I gather it works well. Secondly I have heard of a congregation who regularly have Evensong by playing a record of a well known choir singing the service and they follow in their prayer books and stand and kneel as required. It is hard to imagine this being a regular diet for worship but if it works and the people there find it helpful who am I . . .?

The final alternative is to have unaccompanied singing which works perfectly well provided a note can be given to start everyone off, either on the organ[1] (and somebody must be able to give that) or from one of the worshippers. It is always intriguing to find people who can do this but can't read a note of music!

The second major question of what should be sung depends a great deal on what is feasible. It is imperative to be realistic and to be able as a group to feel that one's singing is actually glorifying God. One congregation of twelve may sing the Magnificat well whereas another . . . In the second instance there is no disgrace in saying canticles. There is sometimes a feeling that feeble chanting is better than nothing because it makes the group believe that they are a proper church. There really cannot be any logic in this view. For example I have often led services with two or three in the congregation in which we have sung two hymns unaccompanied and said the rest and all gone home feeling we have achieved something.

The choice of hymns is important as well. With small numbers it is vital to stick to well known hymns and choruses unless the person leading the music is both confident and competent to teach the congregation new music.

Big festivals

Come Christmas, Easter and Harvest in most situations many will turn up. Some of the regular congregation may resent this and need helping to see that it is better to rejoice at the opportunity it presents. The opportunity is two-fold. Not only have many turned up and thus have a chance to hear the gospel but also the preceding weeks can be a time of preparation for the regular congregation which gives their services definite purpose.

[1] A member of the Group for the Renewal of Worship saw chime bars being used in France for this purpose.

However festivals need not be restricted to the usual ones. There is scope in both town and country situations to include any number of special services which will bring people along. It is possibly easier to do this in the rural setting since villagers may well be expecting something of this nature in the first place. It should be stressed that the aim is not just to provide an opportunity to preach at people but to give people a chance to worship their God!

Service pattern

There needs to be a balance in the monthly service pattern between the varying needs of those who already attend church and those who might be expected to come if something different happened. For example the introduction of a monthly family service[1] can be a definite step of faith for a parish when there are no families coming regularly at the moment. Another difficult issue is deciding how many communion services should be on offer, bearing in mind the reluctance of some to attend communion regularly and of others to attend anything else![2] In a multi-parish benefice the availability of certain key people must be considered including the clergyman, lay readers, organists, bellringers[3] etc.[4]

Leadership

The older people in a village will be able to remember the time when each village had its own parson. Today in rural areas multi-parish benefices are the norm with absurdly large groups of over ten parishes in places. The role of the minister has therefore changed dramatically but a helpful side-effect has been the necessary development of lay ministry. This may ease the pressure on the midweek programme of the clergy but maintaining Sunday service patterns can still be a problem since accredited lay ministry may be in short supply.

Various alternatives exist to try and cope with this problem. In some places weekly services have given way to fortnightly or even monthly services. This is a mistake bearing in mind the previously expressed view that the local church fellowship needs to meet for worship[5] and it is difficult to see how this can be meaningful if nothing takes place more often than once a month.[6]

[1] It may be comparatively easy to encourage interested people to come along to such services. The problem may be the next stage, partly because the 'jump' to attending family communion regularly will at some stage involve confirmation and all that that entails and that is often thought to be a great hurdle.

[2] This is not only to do with churchmanship but with peoples' experiences in the past and so on. There is an interesting discussion of some of the aspects of this issue in Anthony Russell, *op. cit.* ch. 12.

[3] This vital group is often forgotten in service planning but certainly in rural areas people often ring at more than one place on a Sunday morning and many of the ringers will be hoping to worship themselves at some stage along the way.

[4] I have not entered here or anywhere else into a discussion about whether the traditional or modern services are desirable. It is perhaps worth noting that under a monthly pattern some kind of balance is possible if that is what the local church wants.

[5] See above ch. 2.

[6] I have readily conceded that monthly worship may be all that is possible for some individuals—see above p.7.

The other and better alternative is to provide more people to lead the worship and the range is growing. For some time retired clergy, non-stipendiary ministers and lay readers have been available. Now in this diocese there are elders and the prospect of local non-stipendiary ministers as well.[1]

A significant barrier to a proliferation of ministers is the implied idea that they have sufficient time available for all that they are expected to do in this capacity, both on Sundays and during the week. For small congregations it may be better to have worship leaders who are authorized by the bishop and trained locally by the incumbent. Their role would be specifically to take non eucharistic services with no expectation of any pastoral function outside the service.[2]

Preaching

In the rural church described at the start of this booklet[3] the minister was experiencing one of the major difficulties of preaching to small numbers, namely how the sermon can be relevant without being too personal. Adhering fairly rigidly to the lectionary helps because this ensures a measure of objectivity. In turn it will also help if it is known that the lectionary is being followed and why.

Another difficulty is to do with delivery. Should the minister stand in the pulpit? How will the congregation cope without the use of that particular piece of furniture? It is perhaps better to concentrate on the material first and decide from where this is best delivered. It is possibly contemporary not to use the pulpit but sometimes the congregation need to reflect on the subject matter without the proximity of the deliverer of the sermon.

The third danger is that of failing to prepare adequately, for two reasons. Firstly there may be a sneaking thought that the congregation is not worth spending a lot of time over and secondly in multi-parish groups the minister may have several new sermons to prepare each week.[4] However if the preacher thinks that each sermon should be a sermon to oneself as well then all the preparation becomes worthwhile.

---

[1] The author is sceptical about how such people will differ from existing non-stipendiary ministers in practice! It is also questionable whether the person who is very much the 'persona' of a community should be ordained. In a village relationships are often complex and such a person may find it hard to exercise the 'servant like' aspect of ministry if some or even many of the villagers have been employed by him.

[2] I am assuming that they would be leading non-eucharistic services but there is also the question of extended communion—see David Smethurst, *Extended Communion: an Experiment in Cumbria*, (Grove Books, 1986)

[3] See above p.4.

[4] Again it is tempting to think that each congregation should hear the same sermon, to cut down on preparation. But surely each situation is different and the needs of the people expected to be present not the same as elsewhere?